Farm Animals
Dot Marker Book
For Toddler

Guided Big Dots

Test Your Colours Here

Let's Colour The Farm Animals!

Sheep

This page is intentionally left blank for practice.

Cow

This page is intentionally left blank for practice.

Calf

This page is intentionally left blank for practice.

Cat

This page is intentionally left blank for practice.

This page is intentionally left blank for practice.

Rooster

This page is intentionally left blank for practice.

Hen

This page is intentionally left blank for practice.

Chick

This page is intentionally left blank for practice.

Duck

This page is intentionally left blank for practice.

Goose

This page is intentionally left blank for practice.

Duckling

This page is intentionally left blank for practice.

This page is intentionally left blank for practice.

Puppy

This page is intentionally left blank for practice.

Bee

This page is intentionally left blank for practice.

Deer

This page is intentionally left blank for practice.

Donkey

This page is intentionally left blank for practice.

Dove

This page is intentionally left blank for practice.

Fish

This page is intentionally left blank for practice.

Goat

This page is intentionally left blank for practice.

Horse

This page is intentionally left blank for practice.

Foal

This page is intentionally left blank for practice.

Llama

This page is intentionally left blank for practice.

Ox

This page is intentionally left blank for practice.

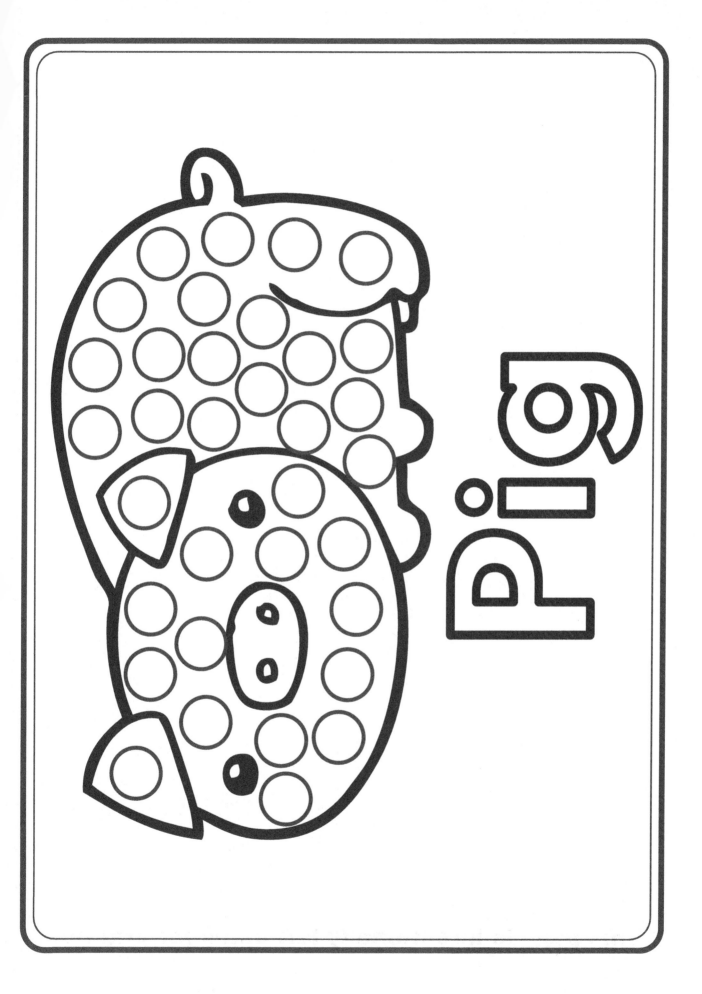

This page is intentionally left blank for practice.

Pigeon

This page is intentionally left blank for practice.

Rabbit

This page is intentionally left blank for practice.

Turkey

This page is intentionally left blank for practice.

Poult

This page is intentionally left blank for practice.

Water Buffalo

This page is intentionally left blank for practice.

Made in the USA
Coppell, TX
24 November 2024